Nabil Eloua...
Nick of Time... ...Ltd present

The Nightmares of Carlos Fuentes

By **Rashid Razaq**

Based on a short story by **Hassan Blasim**

The World Premiere
First performed at the Arcola Theatre Studio 1
on 23 June 2014

Supported by

 BackstageTrust **John S Cohen Foundation** The David&Elaine Potter **Foundation**

AND: Martin Brodie, Ian & Benedicte Clarkson, Baginsky Cohen, Gill Fitzhugh, Jenny Hall, Ali Matar, Nadim & Bobbie Sawalha and The Unity Theatre Trust.

The Nightmares of Carlos Fuentes
By Rashid Razaq

CAST in order of appearance

CARLOS	Nabil Elouahabi
LYDIA	Caroline Langrishe
CASE WORKER/SAHAR	Sara Bahadori
KEVIN/KHALED	Selva Rasalingam

PRODUCTION

Director	Nicolas Kent
Designer	Ellan Parry
Lighting Designer	Matthew Eagland
Sound Designer	Andy Graham
Assistant Director	Diyan Zora
Casting Director	Marilyn Johnson
Production Manager	Andy George
Stage Manager	Sophie Sierra
Assistant Stage Managers	James Enser
	Joanna Walker
	Nicole Vardon
Set Construction	Tim Highman
	& The Scenery Shop
Marketing	EMG Media & Marketing
	(www.emg-ents.com)
Press Representative	Emma Holland
Social Media Manager	Georgia Landers
Cover Design	Shiv Grewal
Production Photographer	Judy Goldhill
General Manager	Mat Burt
Producer	Nicolas Kent
	Nabil Elouahabi
Executive Producers	Heritage Arts Company
	PW Productions
Assistant Producer	Yinka Ayinde
Production Coordinators	Jessica Hall
	Willa Cunningham
Accountant	Jon Catty
	for Nick of Time Productions Ltd
Financial Controller	Bob Thomas
Production Accountant	Dee Vithlami

The play is set in London, an immigration detention centre outside London, and Baghdad between 2006 – 2011.
It runs approximately 75 minutes without an interval.

Acknowledgements

WE ARE VERY GRATEFUL TO THE FOLLOWING INDIVIDUALS, ORGANISATIONS AND COMPANIES FOR THEIR HELP WITH THIS PRODUCTION: SHEENA BHATTESSA , CRESSIDA BROWN, LUCY JACKSON, BEN LATHAM & THE REFUGEE COUNCIL, RICHARD NORTON-TAYLOR, LIZ FRANKEL, RA PAGE, ESTELA WELLDON, PETER WILSON, THE COMMA PRESS, THE MANDEVILLE HOTEL, AND ALL THE STAFF AT THE ARCOLA THEATRE.

HASSAN BLASIM (Writer of the original story)

Is a poet, filmmaker and short story writer. Born in Baghdad in 1973, he studied at the city's Academy of Cinematic Arts, where two of his films 'Gardenia' (screenplay & director) and 'White Clay' (screenplay) won the Academy's Festival Award for Best Work in their respective years. In 1998 he left Baghdad for Sulaymaniya (Iraqi Kurdistan), where he continued to make films, including the feature-length drama *Wounded Camera*, under the pseudonym Ouazad Osman, fearing for his family back in Baghdad under the Hussein dictatorship. In 2004, he moved to Finland, where he has since made numerous short films and documentaries for Finnish television.

His stories have previously been published on www.iraqstory.com and his essays on cinema have featured in Cinema Booklets (Emirates Cultural Foundation). After first appearing in English in *Madinah*, his debut collection *The Madman of Freedom Square* was published by Comma a year later (Nov 2009). *Madman* was long-listed for the Independent Foreign Fiction Prize in 2010, and has since been translated into numerous other languages. A heavily censored Arabic edition was finally published in 2012 and was immediately banned in Jordan. In 2010, Hassan was described by *The Guardian* newspaper as 'perhaps the greatest writer of Arabic fiction alive'. His second collection, *The Iraqi Christ* was published in April 2013, and subsequently translated and published in Finland at the end of 2013. A selection of stories from both of his two collections were published in the States in Feb 2014, by Penguin USA, under the title 'The Corpse Exhibition'. In May 2014, *The Iraqi Christ* was announced the winner of the Independent Foreign Fiction Prize – the first Arabic title ever to win the award and the first short story collection ever to win the award.

RASHID RAZAQ (Playwright)

Rashid's debut play *The President and The Pakistani* (directed by Tom Attenborough), based on the real-life story of Barack Obama and his illegal immigrant flat-mate opened at the Waterloo East Theatre in run-up to the US presidential election in 2012. Rashid's short play *Arab Spring* (starring Nabil Elouahabi) was performed at the Nursery Festival in 2011 and was featured on BBC Arabic Service. His short play, *Hardcore*, was selected for a best of programme at the 503 Theatre. He is a graduate of the Royal Court Theatre's Young Writers' Programme.

Rashid wrote *Man and Boy* (starring Eddie Marsan), which won Best Short at the Tribeca Film Festival 2011 and a top prize at the Aspen Film Festival. His previous short film *Father* (starring Sam Spruell and Matt King) was selected for festivals in the UK and internationally. He has co-written the forthcoming feature film *Orthodox* (starring Stephen Graham) about an Orthodox Jewish boxer and has another feature film in development.

Rashid works as a reporter for the London *Evening Standard* covering subjects including crime, arts and politics, and is a screenwriter as well as a journalist.

CAST

SARA BAHADORI (Case worker/Sahar)

Trained at Bretton Hall, Leeds. She is of Iranian/ British heritage and hails originally from Huddersfield, West Yorkshire. Her television credits include *ITV's Coronation Street, BBC's Waterloo Road, YTV's The Royal Today* and *BBC's Doctors*. Her Theatre credits include *The Worm Collector* at the West Yorkshire Playhouse, *Soul Destroying Finger Food* at The Old Red Lion and *Click* at Riverside Studios. Her comedy work includes performing her own writing in sketch-shows at Leicester Square Theatre and as part of Triforce Promotions' Monologue Slam. Her recent radio work includes impersonating the legendary 'Freda Kelly' as the lead role in *Sorry Boys, You Failed the Audition* for BBC Radio 4. More at www. sarabahadori.com

NABIL ELOUAHABI (Carlos)

Theatre credits include *Love Your Soldiers* at the Sheffield Crucible, *The Great Game: Afghanistan* for the Tricycle Theatre/US Tour, *Crossing Jerusalem* also at the Tricycle and *Sparkleshark* for the National Theatre. Recent Television credits include Fox's *24*, BAFTA award-winning drama *Top Boy* Series II for Channel 4, *Generation Kill* for HBO, *The Path to 9/11* for ABC, *Mad Dogs* on SKY. He is well-known for his role as Tariq in the BBC's *EastEnders* and as GARY in the beloved *Only Fools & Horses*. Film credits include *Zero Dark Thirty*, *Code 46*, *In This World*, *Ali G Indahouse* and *The Sum of All Fears*. *The Nightmares of Carlos Fuentes* will be Nabil's first co-production, with further projects in development.

CAROLINE LANGRISHE (Lydia)

Theatre credits include *The Memory of Water* at the New Vic Theatre/Stephen Joseph Theatre, *The Handyman* at the Yvonne Arnaud Theatre/national tour, *Country* at the Southwark Playhouse, *Hay Fever* at the Chichester Festival Theatre, *Tons of Money* on national tour, *Private Lives* at the Windsor Theatre Royal, *Marrying the Mistress* on a national tour, *Murderer* at the Menier Chocolate Factory, *The Way of the World* at the Manchester Royal Exchange, *Our Song* on national tour, *An Ideal Husband* on national tour, *'Tis Pity She's a Whore* at the Young Vic Theatre, *Twelfth Night* at the Riverside Studios, *Present Laughter* at the Wyndham's Theatre, *Private Lives* and *Talk of The Devil* at the Watford Palace Theatre, *The Philanderer* at the Hampstead Theatre, *The Knickers* at the Lyric Theatre Hammersmith and *A Month in the Country, Don Juan, Much Ado about Nothing,* and *Danton's Death* at the National Theatre. Caroline is best known on screen for roles including Charlotte Cavendish in *Lovejoy*, Georgina Channing in *Judge John Deed* and Marilyn Fox in *Casualty*. Her other screen credits include *Death in Paradise, The Case, Outnumbered, Pete Versus Life, Midsomer Murders, Sharpe, Sons Daughters and Lovers, Poirot, Chancer, Pulaski, Wuthering Heights, Anna Karenina* and *The Glittering Prizes*. Film Credits include *Plastic, Love's Kitchen, Second Son, Bonobo, David Rose, Memorablis, Kisna, Rogue Trader, Newborn, Parting Shots, Crimetime, Twelfth Night, Hawks, Cleopatra, Dead Man's Folly, A Christmas Carol, Les Miserables, Mistral's Daughter Death Watch,* and *The Eagle's Wing*.

SELVA RASALINGAM (Kevin/Khaled)

Theatre credits include Nicolas Kent's productions *The Riots (Tricycle)* and *Guantanamo* (West End transfer); *On the Record* (Ice and Fire Productions/Arcola), *Mary Stuart* (Derby Playhouse), *Eden's Empire* (Finborough), RSC's *Midnight's Children* (US/UK tour and Barbican). TV includes: *Luther, Hustle, Doctor Who, Spooks, Torchwood, Waking the Dead, Jonathan Creek* (BBC); *Joseph* (Turner Pictures/BBC); *The Borgias* (Sky Atlantic); *Run, The Golden Years* by Arthur Miller (Channel 4); *Herod the Great* as Herod (Five); *Londynczycy* (Telewizja Polska); *Law and Order* (ITV). Film includes: Jesus in *The Gospels* film series; *The Veteran, The Devil's Double, Prince of Persia, Skyfall, Man About Dog, Carry on Columbus, Son of the Pink Panther*. Trained at the Guildhall School of Music and Drama.

CREATIVE TEAM

NICOLAS KENT (Director)

Started his career at Liverpool Playhouse in 1967 as an ABC TV trainee regional theatre director. In 1970 he became Artistic Director of the Watermill Theatre, from 1970-72 Associate Director of the Traverse Theatre, Edinburgh and from 1976-81 Administrative Director of The Oxford Playhouse Company. From 1984-2012 he was Artistic Director of the Tricycle Theatre in London.

He has directed productions in over 100 theatres around the world including the West End and New York; as well as for notable companies in Great Britain including The National Theatre, The Royal Shakespeare Company, The Royal Court, The Donmar Warehouse, The Hampstead Theatre, the Lyric Theatre Hammersmith and the Young Vic.

He is probably best known for the political work he did at Tricycle Theatre, where the verbatim plays he directed became known as the Tricycle Tribunal plays, and included *The Colour of Justice (the Stephen Lawrence Inquiry), Nuremberg, Srebrenica, Bloody Sunday* (Olivier Award for Special Achievement), *Guantanamo* & *The Riots*. Most were broadcast by the BBC, and two were performed in the Houses of Parliament and on Capitol Hill. They constituted a body of work which won the *Evening Standard* Theatre Awards Special Award for "pioneering political theatre".

In 2009 directed the nine-hour trilogy *The Great Game – Afghanistan* which was nominated for an Olivier award in London, and subsequently toured the USA; as well as two command performances for the Pentagon in Washington in 2011. One year later he directed an eight play series: *The Bomb: a partial history*

He has also directed many plays in the USA both regionally and in New York, on BBC TV and radio. Most recently he directed David Greig's *Letter of Last Resort* for BBC Radio 4, and his own translation of Jean-Claude Grumberg's *I just don't believe it* with Michael Gambon & Frances de La Tour at the 2013 Cheltenham Literary Festival

He was awarded an Honorary Degree at Westminster University in 2006, the Liberty Human Rights Award 2010 and the first ever Freedom of the Borough of Brent in 2012.

ELLAN PARRY (Designer)

Is a previous winner of the Jocelyn Herbert Award and a Linbury Prize Finalist. Recent designs include *El Niño* (dir. John la Bouchardiere, Spoleto Festival, Charleston, USA), the world premier of new opera *Neige* (dir. Catherine Kontz, Grand Theatre de Ville, Luxembourg), *The Miser,* (dir. Nancy Meckler, Watermill Theatre, Newbury), *Noye's Fludde* (dir. Olivia Fuchs, Southbank Centre, London), *Someone Who'll Watch Over Me,* (dir. Caroline Leslie, the Theatre, Chipping Norton), *The Secret Marriage* (dir. Martin Lloyd-Evans, British Youth Opera, Peacock Theatre, London), *The Fairy Queen* (dir. Susannah Waters, Brighton Theatre Royal), *Without You* (dir. Steve Maler, Menier Chocolate Factory, London, and the Panasonic Theatre, Toronto – co-designer with Timothy Bird), *Electric Hotel* (Fuel/Sadlers Wells, dir. David Rosenberg, national tour – costume designer), *Sense & Sensibility* (dir. Helen Tennison, Yvonne Arnaud Theatre and touring, nominated for Off West End Award – Best Design), and community productions of *Carmen* (dir. James Hurley, Sadlers Wells, London) and *The Magic Flute* (dir. Andrew Leveson, Glyndebourne). Ellan trained at Motley and Wimbledon School of Art.

MATTHEW EAGLAND (Lighting Designer)

Trained at the Guildhall School of Music and Drama, before eventually heading the lighting departments of the Yvonne Arnaud Theatre, Guildford and Cambridge Arts Theatre, and has subsequently designed the lighting for many productions throughout the UK and around the World.

Recent productions include: *Variation on a Theme* and *This Was A man* (both at The Finborough), *Ignis* (The Print Room), *It's a Wonderful Life* (Pitlochry Festival Theatre), *Kindertransport* (National Tour), *September in the Rain* (National Tour), *Mansfield Park* (National Tour), *The West End Men* (The Vaudeville), *I Lombardi* (UCO), Alan Ayckbourn's *Intimate Exchanges* cycle of plays (Mercury Colchester), *Flow* (The Print Room), *Haunting Julia* (Tour), Derren Brown's *Svengali*, *Cool Hand Luke* (Aldwych Theatre), and *Broken Glass* (Vaudeville Theatre).

Other highlights... **Plays**: *Terre Haute* (Trafalgar Studios and 59E59 Theater, New York), *The Secret of Sherlock Holmes* Duchess Theatre, *Our Man in Havana* (Nottingham Playhouse), *Carrie's War* (The Apollo Theatre, Shaftesbury Avenue), *Darwin in Malibu* (Birmingham Rep), *Moon on a Rainbow Shawl* (Nottingham Playhouse), *My Boy Jack* (National tour), *An Hour and a Half Late* (Theatre Royal Bath Productions), *Little Women* (Duchess Theatre) and *Copenhagen* (Watford Palace). **Musicals**: *Assassins, A Little Night Music, Company,*

Grand Hotel (Royal Academy of Music) *Alfie* (Watford Palace) and *Murderous Instincts* (Savoy Theatre). **Opera**: *La Traviata, L Elisir di Amore, La Finta Semplice, Jacko's Hour, The Long Christmas Dinner* and *The Dinner Engagement* (double bill), *L'Heure Espagnol* and *Gianni Schicchi* (double bill).

ANDY GRAHAM (Sound Designer)

Graduated from Mountview Theatre School in 2001 with a BA (Hons) in Technical Theatre. As a sound operator, credits include *The King & I, The Full Monty, Contact, Jerry Springer The Opera* (Olivier Award for Best Sound), *Guys And Dolls* (Olivier Nomination), *The Lord Of The Rings* (Olivier Nomination), *Our House, Loserville* and *Once – The Musical* (Olivier nomination).

For Kneehigh Theatre Company, Andy has worked as an operator and Associate Sound Designer on three seasons of The Asylum, *Brief Encounter* (UK Tour, USA & Australian Tours & Broadway – Tony Nomination for Best Sound), *The Red Shoes* (UK, USA and Australia), *The Wild Bride* (UK, USA and New Zealand), *The King of Prussia, Midnight's Pumpkin,* and *Blast!*

Solo design work and collaborations include *Mary Rose* (Riverside Studios), *Allegro, Spend Spend Spend* (LMST/Bridewell), *Jekyll and Hyde* (English Theatre, Vienna), *A Very Old Man With Enormous Wings* (BAC), *The Kiss Of The Spider Woman* (Arts Ed), *The Other School* (NYMT/St James), *A Scent Of Flowers* (Brockley Jack) and *The Beautiful Game* (Union). He is currently the UK Sound Associate for *Once – The Musical* (Phoenix) and *Handbagged* (Vaudeville).

NICK OF TIME PRODUCTIONS LTD presents politically engaged theatre with the aim of encouraging discussion and debate around important issues, and giving a voice to marginalised groups. The company is run by Nicolas Kent with a broad range of associates including Mary Lauder (former General Manager of the Tricycle Theatre) Jack Bradley (former Literary Manager of the National Theatre and presently working with Sonia Friedman Productions Ltd), Belinda Lang (actor), Nabil Elouahabi (actor), Jenny Jules (actor) and Charlotte Westenra (director).

Since 2012 Nick of Time Productions has commissioned plays from Clare Bayley and Rahila Gupta on deaths in custody in collaboration with Inquest and supported by the Joseph Rowntree Charitable Trust. The company is also working on a project on Drones co-produced with Jemima Khan, and with commissions from Christina Lamb & Ron Hutchinson, David Greig and Amit Gupta.

COMMA PRESS is a Manchester-based publishing 'experiment' specialising in short narratives; it is the most prolific hardcopy publisher of short stories in the UK, and also regularly commissions short film adaptations – poem-films and short story adaptations. For more information go to commapress.co.uk or follow us on Twitter @ commapress.

HERITAGE ARTS COMPANY

The Heritage Arts Company exists to rouse the public imagination, through both creating its own work and producing work by others. We employ spectacle to inform, to entertain and to teach. We are an arts company, undertaking all mediums and art forms, but our home is in live performance. Our guiding principles are equality and honesty. Since 2007 we've made or produced radio plays, straight theatre, modern dance, gallery installations, set design, multiplayer games, and the VAULT Festival – the largest arts festival of its kind in London. Recent work includes VAULT Festival 2014 ("An incredibly rich programme of theatre, music and comedy" – *The Independent*"), the stage adaptation of Hunter S. Thompson's gonzo classic *Fear And Loathing In Las Vegas* ("A real blast... a trip I heartily recommend ★★★★" – *The Telegraph*) and a brand new adaptation of Ian McEwan's debut novel *The Cement Garden,* starring George Mackay and Ruby Bentall ("Adventurous and youthfully energetic ★★★★" – *The Times*). www.heritagearts.co.uk | @HeritageArts | facebook.com/HeritageArtsCompany

PW PRODUCTIONS

PW Productions is one of the West End's most prolific and significant theatre producers, responsible for some of the most successful theatre productions in British theatre over the past 30 years, including *The Woman In Black* and *An Inspector Calls*. We specialise in high-quality production, management and bookkeeping/accountancy services for first-class plays and musicals in the West End, on tour throughout the UK and (given enough notice) throughout the world. We have acted as General Managers, Bookkeepers and Accountants to more than 250 productions in London and throughout the UK. www.pwprods.co.uk | @PWProds

YOUNG PEOPLE'S CREATIVE WRITING WORKSHOPS
around this production co-ordinated and run by

GILLIAN CHRISTIE (Workshop coordinator)

Gillian worked with Nicolas Kent as Education Director at the Tricycle Theatre for over 12 years delivering a variety of creative projects and workshops for children and young people. In addition to facilitating creative writing workshops, she is project leader for a local inter-generational community event leading to Black History Month, and co-ordinating a personal history project for Age UK, both based in Islington.

LUCY POPESCU (Workshop Artistic Director)

Lucy Popescu is a writer, arts critic and creative writing teacher with a background in literature, theatre, and human rights. She is a volunteer mentor with Freedom from Torture's writing group, Write to Life. She runs regular writing workshops in north London and is experienced in inspiring, developing and shaping others' creative work. Lucy is the author of *The Good Tourist* and has edited various books including refugee writer Jade Amoli-Jackson's *Moving a Country*, Write to Life's collection of refugee writing, *Body Maps*, and the PEN anthology *Another Sky*.

THE NIGHTMARES OF CARLOS FUENTES

Rashid Razaq

THE NIGHTMARES OF CARLOS FUENTES

Based on the short story by Hassan Blasim

OBERON BOOKS
LONDON

WWW.OBERONBOOKS.COM

First published in 2014 by Oberon Books Ltd
521 Caledonian Road, London N7 9RH
Tel: +44 (0) 20 7607 3637 / Fax: +44 (0) 20 7607 3629
e-mail: info@oberonbooks.com
www.oberonbooks.com

A catalogue record for this book is available from the British Library.

PB ISBN: 978-1-78319-153-6
E ISBN: 978-1-78319-652-4

Cover design by James Illman

Printed, bound and converted
by CPI Group (UK) Ltd, Croydon, CR0 4YY.

Characters

CARLOS FUENTES (30s)

LYDIA KING (50s)

CASE WORKER/SAHAR HUSAIN

KEVIN/KHALED AL HAMRANI

ONE

August 2007.

A hotel room. A double bed. A chair towards the foot of it. On a bedside table there is a bottle of champagne in an ice bucket.

CARLOS, wearing a hotel dressing gown, is in bed, handcuffed to a bedpost. LYDIA, wearing a slip, is on her hands and knees looking for the key to the handcuffs. Her dress is draped over the chair. A pair of stilettos lie on the floor along with CARLOS' discarded clothes and shoes.

CARLOS is pointing to a spot on the floor with his foot. He has a strong Iraqi accent.

CARLOS: Over there.

LYDIA: Where?

CARLOS: *(Pointing.)* There.

> *She looks to where he is pointing.*

LYDIA: Here?

CARLOS: No. *(His foot can't reach so he indicates with his eyes.)* Look.

LYDIA: *(Looking on the floor.)* I can't see anything.

CARLOS: Look eyes!

LYDIA: What do you think I'm looking with!?

CARLOS: No. Look in my eyes.

LYDIA: In?

CARLOS: My eyes.

LYDIA: *(Confused.)* Your eyes? You want me to look *with* your eyes?

CARLOS: No!

> *CARLOS indicates with his head and eyes.*

LYDIA: Oh! You want me to look *at* your eyes.

CARLOS: Yes!

LYDIA: You're going to try hypnosis?

7

CARLOS: Hypno…what? I want key. What is hip-nose?

LYDIA: It's…never mind. Where am I looking? Show me again.

CARLOS indicates again. LYDIA looks to where he is pointing.

CARLOS: See?

LYDIA: Oh.

CARLOS: Something?

LYDIA: Yes.

LYDIA picks up something from the floor and looks at it.

CARLOS: Is key? *(He pulls at his handcuffs.)* Lydia?

LYDIA: Afraid not. It's your ring.

She gives him the ring. It is a large silver ring with a bright red stone.

CARLOS: Why is this on floor?

LYDIA sits down in the armchair with a sigh. She picks up a glass of champagne and takes a drink.

CARLOS: Who put this here?

LYDIA: Don't look at me.

CARLOS: I put in pocket.

LYDIA: It must have fallen out. Do you want me to keep looking for the key?

CARLOS: Yes, yes. I need to go toilet.

LYDIA: Oh you do, do you?

LYDIA smiles.

CARLOS: Why are you smiling?

LYDIA walks over to CARLOS.

CARLOS: Why are you looking at me like this?

LYDIA jumps on CARLOS and tickles him under the armpits. He lets out a girlish scream. LYDIA tickles him again mercilessly. CARLOS bursts into uncontrollable giggles. LYDIA laughs with glee as she continues to torment her helpless prisoner.

CARLOS: STOP IT PLEASE! I'M GOING TO MAKE WATER! I'M GOING TO... PLEASE LYDIA!

LYDIA relents and gets off the bed. She takes a swig of champagne.

CARLOS: You are terrible, terrible woman!

LYDIA: Only playing darling.

CARLOS: Playing!? I... *(Checks if he pissed himself.)* I almost. What if I make piss in bed? Would you like this?

LYDIA: Well, some people are into that kind of thing.

CARLOS: Uckhh!

LYDIA: They call it watersports.

CARLOS: I don't like to play this sport I think.

LYDIA: Well we could finish the champers and you could go in the bottle.

LYDIA offers the bottle to CARLOS.

CARLOS: I'm not a monkey.

LYDIA: Well, what do you want me to do? I've looked everywhere.

CARLOS: Lydia, please. I don't want to play this game.

LYDIA: OK.

LYDIA finishes her glass and makes to leave.

CARLOS: Where are you going?

LYDIA: To reception. See if they've got something to get you out. Failing that we'll have to call the fire brigade.

CARLOS: I don't want anyone to see me like this.

LYDIA shrugs. She picks up her stilettos and puts on her left shoe. She goes to put on her right shoe. The key falls out. She picks it up and turns around slowly to show CARLOS.

CARLOS: Thank God!

LYDIA releases CARLOS. He leaps out of bed and runs to the bathroom off-stage. The sound of CARLOS relieving himself.

CARLOS returns beaming.

LYDIA: Better?

CARLOS: Much better.

LYDIA pours CARLOS a glass and hands it to him. She refills her glass.

LYDIA: A toast.

CARLOS: To our one month anniversary?

LYDIA: It can't be an anniversary if it's less than a year. To a... work in progress.

LYDIA touches glasses with CARLOS.

CARLOS: Work?

LYDIA: Yes.

CARLOS: I am working?

LYDIA: No. *You're* the work. Do you understand?

Beat.

CARLOS: Yes. Yes. Of course I understand.

LYDIA takes a drink and sits down on the bed. She pats the bed for CARLOS to join her, but he is busy looking inside his rucksack.

LYDIA: What are you doing?

CARLOS takes out a book – The History of The British Isles.

CARLOS: Working.

LYDIA: That's not what I meant.

CARLOS: I must study for test.

CARLOS opens the book and starts reading. LYDIA snatches the book.

CARLOS: Oy!

LYDIA: You can't sit the citizenship test for another four years.

CARLOS: Four years? But I am ready now! Ask me question. I will show. I am Britishman best as you.

LYDIA: Carlos?

CARLOS: Yes.

LYDIA: This is a dirty weekend, yes?

CARLOS: Yes.

LYDIA: I paid good money for this hotel room, yes?

CARLOS: Yes.

LYDIA: So get in the fucking bed.

CARLOS: But darling, I want to make progress.

LYDIA: Bed.

Pause.

CARLOS tries to grab the book. LYDIA pulls it away.

CARLOS: Hah! Sssh! Lydia! You promise you help me. How can I be Britishman if I do not pass test?

Pause.

LYDIA: OK. Five minutes. That's it. *(Reading from the book.)* An inspirational leader to the British people during the Second World War?

CARLOS: Winston Church-hill.

LYDIA: Correct. Name the British queen who fought against the Romans.

CARLOS: *(Uncertain.)* Bod-ica?

LYDIA: Boudica. Or Boudicea. But correct. *(Reading.)* Who is the eleventh-century English king who…

CARLOS: I know this. I know this. *(Beat.)* King Cunt.

LYDIA: Can-oot. King Canute. Cunt means…something else.

CARLOS: Oh. I see. What is next? Come. Test me.

LYDIA: Feeling confident are we?

CARLOS: Maybe.

LYDIA: You've clearly been doing your homework. How about we make it more interesting? How about for every question you get wrong, you have to remove an item of clothing.

CARLOS: But I'm not wearing anything under this dressing gown.

LYDIA: Well, you better not get any wrong then.

LYDIA smiles. CARLOS smiles. She looks at the book.

LYDIA: Let's see. When was the Magna Carta?

CARLOS: 1215.

LYDIA: When was the Battle of Agincourt?

CARLOS: 1415.

LYDIA: Who was the English king who defeated the French?

CARLOS: Henry Vee?

LYDIA: Fifth. It's Henry the Fifth.

CARLOS: Oh. Come Lydia. This is too easy. Ask me something only a British would know.

LYDIA: You are feeling confident. OK. *(Flicking through the book.)* Henry the Eighth. That's Henry with a V and three ones. Who are his six wives?

CARLOS: All of them?

LYDIA: Yes.

CARLOS: They do not ask this on the test.

LYDIA: Well, I'm asking you. Don't you know?

   Beat.

CARLOS: Catherine Aragon.

LYDIA: Correct.

CARLOS: Anne Bol-een.

LYDIA: Boleyn.

CARLOS: Catherine Aragon. Anne Boleyn. Jane Seymours?

LYDIA: Three down.

CARLOS: Anne…Anne Cleeves?

LYDIA: Very good. Two more to go.

CARLOS: Catherine… *(Beat.)* Howard!

LYDIA: Last one.

CARLOS: It is another Catherine.

LYDIA: Yes. But who?

CARLOS: Um…

LYDIA: Don't know?

CARLOS: No. I know.

Beat.

LYDIA: Take it off.

CARLOS: I know this.

LYDIA: Take it off Carlos.

CARLOS: Wait. Wait… *(Beat.)* OK. I will take it off.

LYDIA smiles.

CARLOS puts his hand on his dressing gown cord to undo it. He comes in close to LYDIA.

CARLOS: Parr. Catherine Parr. Is Henry the Eighth's six wife.

LYDIA: You bastard.

They laugh. They kiss. LYDIA takes the bottle of champagne from the ice bucket and takes a swig. She comes over and hands it to CARLOS. He takes the bottle from her and tries to pull her close, but she coquettishly pulls away and walks over to the opposite side of the stage.

They look at each other.

CARLOS takes a swig from the bottle without breaking eye contact with LYDIA.

CARLOS: Darling?

LYDIA: Yes.

CARLOS: This is dirty weekend yes?

LYDIA: Bit clean so far if you ask me.

CARLOS: Yes. What if we do something *different?*

LYDIA: How do you mean?

CARLOS: What if. *(Beat.)* I was boss?

CARLOS picks up the handcuffs and a blindfold and dangles them in front of LYDIA.

LYDIA: Something *different?*

CARLOS: What do you think?

Beat.

LYDIA: Why not?

LYDIA moves over to the bed.

LYDIA: How do you want me?

CARLOS: On your knees. Please.

CARLOS starts handcuffing her.

LYDIA: Ow!

CARLOS: Sorry. It is too tight?

LYDIA: No. It's my knee. Could you pass me a pillow please?

CARLOS places a pillow under LYDIA's right knee. He picks up the blindfold and goes to put it on her.

LYDIA: What do you want me to do when you put it on?

CARLOS: To do what I say. *(Beat.)* If that is OK with you?

LYDIA: Yes, yes. Put it on then.

CARLOS starts to put the blindfold on LYDIA.

LYDIA: Oh! What's the code word?

CARLOS: Code word?

LYDIA: If I want you to stop. *(Beat.)* Agincourt. If I say Agincourt you stop.

CARLOS: OK.

CARLOS puts the blindfold on LYDIA. He stands back and watches her. He takes a sip of champagne.

Pause.

LYDIA: Carlos? *(Beat.)* Hello? *(Pause.)* Car-los? Are you there?

CARLOS comes in close to her ear.

CARLOS: I am not Carlos.

LYDIA: Oh. Who are…

CARLOS: Be quiet. You only talk when I say you talk.

LYDIA: Oh. OK. I understand. Sorry.

CARLOS: Stop talking.

14

LYDIA: OK!

CARLOS runs his hand up her leg.

LYDIA: Oh. Oh! Mmmm.

CARLOS: You like that? Answer me. Do you like that?

LYDIA: Yes. I like it.

CARLOS: Good.

CARLOS rubs up and down both her legs.

LYDIA: It's very nice.

CARLOS: Did I say you could talk?

CARLOS lightly spanks LYDIA's bottom

LYDIA: *(Excited squeal.)* Oh!

CARLOS: That's for being a bad girl.

LYDIA: Oh I deserve it. I'm a bad girl. I'm a very, very bad girl.

CARLOS spanks her bottom twice more. Each spank is met with an excited squeal.

LYDIA: Oh yes. Yes! Punish me. Spank me. I deserve to be punished. Spank me…what's your name?

CARLOS: I am going to do whatever I want to you. And you will never find out who I am.

LYDIA: Oh. That sounds. *(Beat.)* Hot!

CARLOS: You have been a bad girl Lydia.

LYDIA: Yes. I've been very bad.

He spanks her bottom. She moans in pleasure.

CARLOS: And now you must be punished.

LYDIA: Punish me.

He spanks her bottom. She moans.

CARLOS: You're a sexy bitch.

LYDIA: What?

He spanks her bottom.

CARLOS: A dirty bitch.

LYDIA: *(Unsure.)* Dirty?

> *He spanks her bottom.*

CARLOS: A dirty, fucking, white bitch.

LYDIA: Hold on a second.

CARLOS: You're a dirty, fucking, old, white bitch.

> *CARLOS lifts up his hand to spank her.*

LYDIA: WHAT!? WHAT DID YOU JUST SAY!?

CARLOS: What?

LYDIA: What did you just call me?

CARLOS: Nothing.

LYDIA: Agincourt. AGINCOURT! Take this off. Let me see.

> *CARLOS takes off LYDIA's blindfold.*

LYDIA: Uncuff me.

> *CARLOS takes off her handcuffs. LYDIA gets off the bed.*

LYDIA: *Old?*

CARLOS: No. You are…middle-aged.

LYDIA: Excuse me?

CARLOS: No. I mean… I mean you're…you are…

LYDIA: Old?

CARLOS: That is not what I meant.

LYDIA: Why did you say it?

CARLOS: I…it wasn't. Are you sure I said this?…

LYDIA: Yes! You said. You dirty fucking. *Old.* White bitch. That's exactly what you said.

CARLOS: But it wasn't real.

LYDIA: I imagined it?

CARLOS: No, what I mean… I mean the words. The words were not real.

LYDIA: Oh I see. You were faking the words?

CARLOS: Yes! Exactly! I was fucking the words.

LYDIA: *Fake!* Not fuck!

CARLOS: Yes! Exactly!

LYDIA: Fake means not real. Pretend.

CARLOS: Yes, yes. I know. I was…pretending to…be somebody else.

LYDIA: Oh really? Who? Some sort of horrible sexist, racist, ageist prick?

Beat.

CARLOS: *(Unsure.)* Yes?

LYDIA: Why would you do that? Do you think I want to have sex with somebody else?

CARLOS: *(Unsure.)* No?

LYDIA: *No.* Do you?

CARLOS: Yes. No. *No!* Definitely one hundred per cent no. It was…pretend. I was…acting.

LYDIA: I see. So you don't really think I'm a dirty, fucking, old white bitch?

CARLOS: No. Of course not. *(Beat.)* You don't like to play this game I think?

LYDIA gives him a withering look.

CARLOS: Lydia. Darling. Please. I stopped when you told me to stop. When you said Agincourt. I did *not* force you. *(Pause.)* Lydia? *(Beat.)* I did not force you.

LYDIA looks at CARLOS.

Pause.

LYDIA: No.

CARLOS laughs nervously from relief. He tries to lighten the mood.

CARLOS: I'm sorry. I'm sorry. I apologise. I would never. *Never* do…

LYDIA: Let's go to bed. *(Beat.)* To sleep.

Pause.

They get ready for bed.

CARLOS: *(Under his breath.)* Cunt.

LYDIA: What?

CARLOS: Canute. King Canute. Eleventh-century English king. *(Beat.)* Come. Let us sleep.

Pause.

Lights down.

TWO

October 2006.

Immigration detention centre. Two chairs. A table. CARLOS is pacing. He is wearing his ring.

CASE WORKER, female, enters.

CASE WORKER: Please take a seat.

> *They sit.*

CASE WORKER: So Mr… *(Reading from a file.)* Husain. There are some inconsistencies in your asylum application which is why it has been passed to me. *(Beat.)* Do you understand what I'm saying? *(Slower.)* Do you speak English Mr Husain?

> *CARLOS has a strong Iraqi accent.*

CARLOS: Yes.

CASE WORKER: *(Slow.)* How good is your English?

CARLOS: Good.

CASE WORKER: *(Slow.)* It's good is it? Are you sure?

CARLOS: Yes. Good.

CASE WORKER: Good. It's just that we don't want to get half-way through the interview and then you decide you need a translator. Because that would mean we'd have to start all over again from the beginning because your answers would be inadmissible. *(Slow.)* Do you understand what inadmissible means Mr Husain?

> *Beat.*

CARLOS: No.

CASE WORKER: It means that if your asylum application were to be rejected hypothetically. You would…do you know what hypothetically means Mr Husain?

> *Beat.*

CARLOS: No.

CASE WORKER: For example. It means for example. Say that *for example* your asylum application were to be rejected. But then you claimed you didn't understand the questions because we didn't provide you with a translator. It would mean that I got into trouble with my boss. You wouldn't want me to get into trouble with my boss would you Mr Husain?

CARLOS: No. Of course no.

CASE WORKER: OK. So let's proceed and see how we get on…

CARLOS: He is terrible?

CASE WORKER: Who?

CARLOS: Your boss. He is bad man? He will beat you?

CASE WORKER: No. My boss is a woman.

CARLOS: Ah. Your boss is woman.

CASE WORKER: Yes. So.

CARLOS: This is good. To have bosses who can be women.

CASE WORKER: Yes. In Britain we have lots of women bosses.

CARLOS: And this is why I come Britain. Here equal. In Iraq no equal. But in Britain. Equal.

CASE WORKER: Yes. We believe in equality here. So your full name is Salim Abdul Husain. Born… Baghdad..

CARLOS: And free.

CASE WORKER looks up.

CARLOS: Britain is free also.

CASE WORKER: Yes. What I need to know is…

CARLOS: It is land of the free is it not?

CASE WORKER: Yes. I suppose so.

CARLOS: The land of the free. *(Beat.)* And the home of the brave.

CASE WORKER: No, no. That's America. You're getting us mixed up.

CARLOS: Ah. Britain is not home of brave?

CASE WORKER: No…

CARLOS: Oh. So what Britain home of?

CASE WORKER: It's just…

CARLOS: The just! Britain is home of the just!

CASE WORKER: Um…no. That's not right either.

CARLOS: What is Britain?

CASE WORKER struggles to answer.

Beat.

CASE WORKER: Can we press on please Mr Husain? We've got a lot to get through here and I do have other people to see.

CARLOS: Yes. Yes. Please. Continue.

CASE WORKER: So you entered the UK three weeks ago?

CARLOS: Correct.

CASE WORKER: Point of entry Dover.

CARLOS: Yes.

CASE WORKER: By lorry.

CARLOS: This is true.

CASE WORKER: In fact you were discovered inside a frozen goods vehicle by customs officers.

CARLOS: Peas.

CASE WORKER: What?

CARLOS: Peeese.

CASE WORKER: Please? *(Slowly.)* I don't understand what you're saying.

CARLOS: Small. Green. *(Searching for the correct word.)* Vegetable.

CASE WORKER: Oh you mean peas! You were in a lorry carrying frozen peas.

CARLOS: Yes. It was. *(Pretends to shiver.)* Very cold.

CASE WORKER: So your route from Iraq was overland?

CARLOS: Yes.

CASE WORKER: Which countries did you pass through?

CARLOS: Ah. Turkey. Greece. Albania. Serbia. Hungary. Austria. Italia. France. And Britain.

CASE WORKER: I see. So why didn't you claim asylum in any of those countries? Why did you wait until you got to Britain?

CARLOS: Truth? *(Beat.)* I was sleeping.

CASE WORKER: You were asleep?

CARLOS: Yes.

CASE WORKER: You passed through. *(Reading.)* One, two, three, four, five, six, seven countries and you were asleep the whole time. That's what you're telling me?

CARLOS: I am very…deep sleep. When I was child they say you can not wake Salim. He is sleeping like dead. Dead! You can not wake dead persons. It is joke. Maybe we should get translator.

CASE WORKER: No. I get it. What you're telling me sounds incredible.

CARLOS: Thank you.

CASE WORKER: No! Not in a good way. I mean I find it hard to believe that you felt your life was in danger but you passed through seven countries, five European Union member states, to reach Britain before claiming asylum. *(Beat.)* I don't believe you Mr Husain.

CARLOS: I am telling you truth.

CASE WORKER notices CARLOS' ring.

CASE WORKER: That's a nice ring. Looks valuable.

CARLOS smiles.

CASE WORKER: You're fleeing persecution in Iraq Mr Husain?

CARLOS: Persecution yes.

CASE WORKER: Do you know what the definition of persecution is Mr Husain?

CARLOS: Yes. *(Beat.)* No. What is definition?

CASE WORKER: It means your life is in danger.

CARLOS: Yes. Yes. My life in big danger. My family in danger.

CASE WORKER: I thought you travelled here alone.

CARLOS: I did. I had to leave them.

CASE WORKER: Why is your life in danger in Iraq?

CARLOS: I am member of religious…minority. Yes.

CASE WORKER: Which religious minority are you a member of? *(Beat.)* Are you a Sunni?

CARLOS: No.

CASE WORKER: A Shia?

CARLOS: No. Not Shia.

CASE WORKER: What then? Christian? Jewish? What are you?

CARLOS: I am atheist.

CASE WORKER: An atheist?

CARLOS: Yes. I have not always been atheist. No. No one is born atheist. Not in Iraq anyway. But since April. I have been. Atheist.

CASE WORKER: And that's why your life is in danger? Because you're an atheist?

CARLOS: Yes. Correct.

CASE WORKER: Because you're…unable to practise your beliefs?

CARLOS: How do you mean practise?

CASE WORKER: Observe. *Perform.* You are unable to perform your beliefs?

CARLOS: What is there to perform? I am atheist.

CASE WORKER: So you're being compelled…forced to act not in accordance with your beliefs?

CARLOS: I don't have beliefs. I told you. I am atheist.

CASE WORKER: Are they making you…for example. Are they making you go to a mosque or a church? Something of that nature?

CARLOS: Who?

CASE WORKER: Whoever is persecuting you.

CARLOS: *(Laughing.)* Nobody is forcing me to go to a mosque. Or a church.

CASE WORKER: So who are you afraid of?

CARLOS: Ah. *(Beat.)* God.

CASE WORKER: I thought you didn't believe in God.

CARLOS: I don't.

CASE WORKER: But you're living in fear of him?

CARLOS: Yes. Very much so.

CASE WORKER: You don't believe God exists but yet you are living in fear of him?

CARLOS: I don't say I don't think God exists.

CASE WORKER: That's what an atheist is Mr Husain. Maybe we do need a translator…

CARLOS: Unbeliever! Unbeliever. That is what I meant. Yes. Of course God exists. How can God not exist? That is like saying this table does not exist. Or these chairs do not exist. Or you or I do not exist.

CASE WORKER: Well we can see those things Mr Husain. They are *real.*

CARLOS: Yes. But we can not see…air. Oxygen. That we can not see. Or fear. Or anger. Or love. We can not see those things but nobody is saying they not exist. No. God exists. I am refusing to…believe in him. I am an unbeliever. The problem is. Iraq is not a safe place for an unbeliever. There are many hazards. A car bomb. An American soldier. A neighbour who likes the look of your wife's thighs. There are many ways for God to get a unbeliever in Iraq. That is why I wanted to come somewhere where God can not find me.

CASE WORKER: That's why you want to live in Britain?

CARLOS: Yes. *(Smiling.)* Somewhere really godless. With lots of unbelievers.

CASE WORKER: I see.

CARLOS: Somewhere it is going to be difficult for him to find me. But I was thinking. If possible. To change my name.

CASE WORKER: Change your name to what?

CARLOS: Well, I know God spends a lot of time in Iraq and the Middle East is his base generally, but they say he has branches everywhere. So I thought Salim why not change your name to something not Arab? You know. Make it extra difficult for him to find you. Throw him off the stink. But which name? Obviously it not be too British. Not Tony or Gordon. It needs to be a brown name. I was. *(Taking out a torn page from a magazine.)* I was reading this magazine outside and I saw this article. What do you think of? *(Slowly.)* Carlos Fuentes.

CASE WORKER: Carlos Fuentes?

CARLOS: Yes. Carlos Fuentes.

CASE WORKER: Who is Carlos Fuentes?

CARLOS: I don't know. I didn't actually read the article. I think he is Spanish or Mexican or something. But look at his picture. Look! He has the same complexion as me. Burnt barley bread. And he has a nice face. Kind eyes. Yes. Carlos Fuentes is name for me I think. My lucky name.

CASE WORKER: So let me just get this correct Mr Husain…

CARLOS: Please. Mr Fuentes.

CASE WORKER: Mr…in this box where it asks for a reason for seeking asylum in Britain. You want me to write fleeing persecution from God?

CARLOS: Yes. That would be correct.

CASE WORKER: I see.

CARLOS: And this form will go direct to President Bear?

CASE WORKER: President? Bear? You mean Blair? Tony Blair? The Prime Minister?

CARLOS: Yes. It will go for his attention?

Beat.

CASE WORKER: Yes. But I think you may struggle if we wrote God on this application form. You see the last time I checked, God wasn't on the Home Office's recognised dictators list. But there is this other box here. Which asks if you've ever been diagnosed with a mental illness. *(Beat.)* Say *for example* your life was in danger because you couldn't get the medical treatment you require in your country of origin, then that *could* be a reason to grant you leave to remain. On compassionate grounds. We are home to the compassionate. *(Beat.)* What do you think Mr… *(Beat.)* God or insanity?

Pause.

Blackout.

THREE

July 2007.

A Lebanese restaurant. Arabic music plays. LYDIA sits alone nursing a drink and watching the dancefloor.

CARLOS, dressed in a waiter's uniform, approaches carrying a tray full of drinks. He is wearing his ring and has a strong Iraqi accent.

CARLOS: Ah madam. Your drinks. A small red wine. A large white wine. A white wine spritzer. A double gin and tonic. A… *(Studies a bizarre-looking green cocktail.)* something. And a pint of lager.

LYDIA: They're not all for me.

CARLOS: Sorry?

LYDIA: *(Smiling.)* My friends are dancing downstairs. I don't want you to think I'm an alcoholic or something.

CARLOS: *(Slightly confused.)* No. Of course no. Will there be anything else?

LYDIA: What's your name?

CARLOS: My name?

LYDIA: Yes.

CARLOS: My name is Carlos. *(Pointing at his name tag.)* It is written here.

LYDIA: That's an unusual name for a Lebanese person.

CARLOS: *(Smiling.)* Yes. It would be. But I am not Lebanese. I am from Mexico.

LYDIA: Ah, hablas Espanol?

CARLOS: *(Smiling.)* Si.

LYDIA: Te gusta vivir aqui? De donde eres en México?

CARLOS: Si. *(Beat.)* Si. No, well actually I don't speak Spanish. I am Mexican. But I grew up in Iraq.

LYDIA: Oh. Interesting.

CARLOS: Yes. My father was oil engineer. We moved to Iraq
for his job. The money was good, but I got this horrible
Arabic accent. I don't like it. I want to sound like a British.

LYDIA: I like your accent.

CARLOS: *(Surprised.)* You like the sound of Arabic? It sounds
like pigs making children. It is not nice. Dirty. *(Makes
guttural sounds.)* Like you have a cold and are trying to
clear your breast. *(Makes sounds.)*

LYDIA laughs.

LYDIA: I envy you. I can speak a little French. A smattering
of Spanish. Neither of them very well. We're not good at
learning other languages. English people.

CARLOS: Why would you want to speak any other language?
English is the greatest language in the world.

LYDIA: Well, it's the most widely-spoken. But I don't know if
you can call it the greatest. What makes a language great?
It's all rather subjective don't you think?

CARLOS doesn't understand.

LYDIA: A lot of people would say French sounds nicer. Is more
romantic than English. I suppose you could say the same
about Italian or Spanish. But even that's quite a European
view. What's to say one language is intrinsically better or
worse than any other language? Why not Arabic? They say
we'll all be speaking Mandarin soon anyway.

CARLOS: Arabic is a backward……primitive……language.
The Arabs they are a backward, primitive people. Not
even people really. Savage tribes. But English. Ah. English
is the language of democracy, of equality, of freedom, of…

LYDIA: Power?

CARLOS: I am sorry. I should go.

LYDIA: Don't. Sit with me.

CARLOS: I am not allowed to sit.

LYDIA: What? Ever?

LYDIA smiles. CARLOS smiles.

CARLOS: To sit with customers. It will make trouble with my boss.

LYDIA: Is he a slave driver? Your boss?

CARLOS: It is a she. *(Looks over his shoulder for his boss.)* Yes. She is big slave driver.

LYDIA: What if I asked you to stand?

CARLOS: If that is what the customer wishes.

LYDIA: The customer would like to talk to you.

CARLOS: You don't want to bellydance with your friends downstairs?

LYDIA: They're not my friends. They're my colleagues. Or employees to be precise. Besides, I'm too old to bellydance.

CARLOS: Yes. You are.

LYDIA laughs.

CARLOS: What is funny?

LYDIA: You.

CARLOS: Why? What I say?

LYDIA: Oh. Nothing. It's my birthday today.

CARLOS: Happy Birthday!

LYDIA: I'm fifty-s(ix.)...how old are y(ou.)...no. Don't. It's refreshing to hear somebody say what they really think. You haven't been here long enough to pick up our bad habits.

CARLOS: I would like to be British. To be a Britishman.

LYDIA: Not even the British particularly want to be British anymore.

CARLOS: I am not like these other foreigners. These immigrants. Working here illegally. Not paying taxes. Not respecting the law. Always complaining about Britain and the British. Hating the people who have fed them and housed them. They are retarded......gerbils.

LYDIA: Gerbils?

CARLOS: Stone Age savages. *I* am not like them!

LYDIA: I believe you.

CARLOS: I have had too much misery and war and death and shit and piss and camels. I want a country that treats me with respect so that I can worship it and believe in it. A country with streets clean and green trees. With peace and soft toilet paper. Where a girl in a short skirt can walk across the road without getting gobbled up by the ground. I want to change my skin and my blood. Let my lungs breathe clean, pure British air.

Beat.

LYDIA: It sounds like you want to rebrand yourself.

CARLOS: What does this mean?

LYDIA: You want to change the way people perceive you? See you.

CARLOS: Yes.

LYDIA: Maybe I can help. I run a marketing company. Lydia King Communications? *(Beat.)* I advise companies who want to project a...certain image of themselves.

CARLOS: Why do you do this?

LYDIA: Well. For money. *(Smiling.)* It pays rather well. But so they can sell more of their products. You see Carlos if you want to rebrand yourself you need to think of yourself as a company with something to sell. What are you trying to sell? What have you got to offer?

CARLOS: *(Confused.)* I don't understand.

LYDIA: What is your USP? Your Unique Selling Point? The thing that is going to appeal to the consumer. Imagine I'm the consumer and you're trying to sell me your...car. Why should I buy your car?

CARLOS: *(Confused.)* But I don't have a car.

LYDIA laughs.

CARLOS: Sorry.

LYDIA: *(Breathily.)* Carlos?

CARLOS: Yes.

LYDIA: Tell me about you.

CARLOS: What do you want to know?

LYDIA: What are you into?

CARLOS: I don't understand.

LYDIA: What do you enjoy doing?

CARLOS: Many things.

LYDIA: Like what?

CARLOS: I…like to surf the internet.

LYDIA: You see if you were my client, I could say for example that you have a lovely smile. Or sexy eyes. But then that would only be the superficial, surface level. I'd have to delve deeper to find out who you really are.

CARLOS: I am Carlos Fuentes.

LYDIA smiles.

LYDIA: What are your hidden talents Carlos Fuentes? What should the world know about you?

CARLOS: I'm good at fixing things.

LYDIA: You're good with your hands?

She reaches out and takes his hand. She sees the ring.

LYDIA: You're married.

CARLOS: No. It is…my family…

LYDIA: A family heirloom?

CARLOS: *(Confused.)* Air?

LYDIA: Hair.

CARLOS: Hair?

LYDIA: Loom.

Beat.

CARLOS: *(Smiling.)* Yes. Your hair look nice.

LYDIA: Never mind. Tell me about you Carlos.

CARLOS: I read magazines if they have been left behind. Something like this?

LYDIA: God, you're not making this easy for me Carlos.

CARLOS: Make what?

LYDIA: I'm trying to pick you up.

CARLOS: Pick me up for what?

LYDIA: What do you think? *(Beat.)* Sex.

CARLOS: Sex? Me and you?

LYDIA: Yes.

CARLOS smirks.

LYDIA: I get it.

CARLOS: Get what?

LYDIA: You think it's amusing?

CARLOS: *(Smirking.)* A little. Yes.

LYDIA: That you'd be interested in me.

CARLOS: Oh, no, no. That is not what I was laughing at. To hear you say that in public. A woman. Sex.

CARLOS smirks.

CARLOS: It is funny because you mean sexual intercourse.

LYDIA: If you're not interested I understand. Really. It's got a little awkward now.

CARLOS: No. I am interested. How does this work? It is my first time.

LYDIA: You're a virgin?

CARLOS: No! With a Britishwoman. My first time in this country. How do we do it? You give me your number. I call you. We go to a restaurant. Roses. Some disco dancing. Yes?

LYDIA: Well, we're already in a restaurant. Why don't we just cut to the chase? *(Beat.)* What time do you finish?

CARLOS: You are the last table. Right after you pay the bill.

LYDIA goes into her handbag and takes out her credit card from her purse. She hands it to CARLOS.

CARLOS: Will there be anything else?

LYDIA takes out a bundle of £20 notes from her purse and hands it to CARLOS.

LYDIA: Your tip.

CARLOS: Thank you. *(Beat.)* I'll go and fetch your coat.

Pause.

Lights down.

INTERLUDE 1

July 2007.

During the scene change SAHAR walks onstage talking into a mobile phone.

SAHAR: *(Phone.)* Salim. Salam-alaikum. Yes. Yes. She is here. One second. I will call her. *(Off.)* Lina! *(Crouching down as if beckoning a small child.)* Come. *(Phone.)* She won't come. *(Off.)* Lina. Come talk to him. *(Phone.)* She says she doesn't want to talk. *(Beat.)* No. *No.* She has not forgotten you. Why would you think that? *(Smiles off.)* She is being shy. *(Beat.)* No. I have not forgotten you either. *(Pause.)* I miss you too. *(Beat.)* Yes. We got the money. I don't know. I don't know when. My father is not any better. Huh? Well why do you always ask the same thing then? *(Beat.)* I don't know. Nothing has changed. *(Beat.)* Goodbye.

She ends the call and leaves.

FOUR

July 2011.

Heathrow Airport. Holding room. A table. Two chairs. Stark light. CARLOS is asleep in his chair, his head slumped forward. His hands are handcuffed together. He has no ring and a slight Iraqi accent.

KEVIN, a burly, heavy-set private security guard is sat opposite. KEVIN is dressed in black polyester trousers and a half-sleeve white shirt with a clip-on tie. He is looking inside a rucksack placed on his lap.

CARLOS begins to stir in his sleep. KEVIN hears CARLOS and looks up from the bag. CARLOS wakes with a jolt. He is dry-mouthed and groggy, appearing slow and bewildered as if he has been drugged.

KEVIN has a strong Geordie accent and a friendly demeanour despite his somewhat intimidating appearance.

KEVIN: *(Smiling.)* Hallo Sleeping Beauty. Back with us in the land of the living?

CARLOS looks confused. He tries to speak, but his mouth is dry and his voice is weak.

CARLOS: *(Weak.)* What…

KEVIN: Would you like a drink a water? *(Takes out a bottle of water from his bag and walks over.)* Come on. Let's have a drink a water.

KEVIN goes to put the bottle to CARLOS' lips. CARLOS pulls away and tries to reach for the bottle himself, but realises his hands are cuffed.

CARLOS: *(Weak.)* Why…

KEVIN: What's that?

CARLOS grabs the bottle and takes a drink.

Pause.

CARLOS: Why am I in handcuffs?

KEVIN sighs and sits back down.

KEVIN: Are we gonna have to go through this rigmarole again? *(Shakes his head and smiles.)* 'E, honestly. It's every time with you. *(Slowly as if he is speaking to a child.)* My name's Kevin. *Your* name's Salim. *I'm* a security guard. *You* are a prisoner. *We* are at Heathrow Airport.

CARLOS looks confused as he takes it all in.

CARLOS: I was asleep.

KEVIN: That's right. *(Slowly.) You* were asleep. You was having a little snooze.

CARLOS: I don't remember…what am I doing here?

KEVIN: Don't worry. It'll come back to ya. You're always a bit woozy when ya wake up. Cos a ya medication.

The airport tannoy system cuts in. The voice is female, English and received pronunciation.

KEVIN stops to listen.

TANNOY: Boarding call for American Airlines flight AA15 to New York. Boarding now at gate seven.

KEVIN: Not us. Are ya hungry? I divn't knaa about ye but I'm always a bit peckish when a wake up from a nap. I've got… *(Looks in his bag and takes out food.)* I've got sandwiches. There's ham and cheese. Or there's *(Reading box.)* Mediterranean-style crunchy tuna. Nah? *(Taking it out.)* Salt and vinegar Hula Hoops? Or…or a banana? *(Pulls out an over-ripe banana.)* It's a bit black like, but it'll be alreet if ya take the top off. *(Beat.)* Nah? It'll be a while till the feed us on the plane. *(Beat.)* Aye, well just let us knaa if ya change ya mind. They're in me bag. Here? Salim? What d'ya reckon to these sunglasses?

KEVIN roots around in his bag.

CARLOS: Where's…

KEVIN takes out a pair of Oakley sunglasses, puts them on and turns to face CARLOS.

KEVIN: The Oakleys? Or the…

KEVIN takes off the Oakleys and looks inside his bag.

CARLOS: Where's my…

KEVIN puts on a pair of Ray-Ban sunglasses.

KEVIN: Or the Ray-Bans? *(Taking them off.)* Tell the truth. It's the Oakleys isn't it? The Ray-Bans are too big for me heed. I look like a Russian cosmonaut gannin to the moon…

CARLOS: Where is my wife?…

KEVIN: That's ten pund doon the drain.

CARLOS: Where is my wife?

KEVIN: I don't know.

CARLOS: Please. Can I call her? She will come for me.

KEVIN: No. She won't.

CARLOS: Please. Can I speak to her?

KEVIN: No. You can't. Ya not allowed to contact her.

CARLOS: Why?

KEVIN: Jesus! Maybe cos you violently assaulted her.

CARLOS: I don't remember.

KEVIN: *(Smiling.)* Didn't stand up in court did it?

CARLOS: Why can't I remember?

KEVIN: Ya medication. For ya nightmares. So ya can sleep without having those bad dreams that make ya gan all *(Does the crazy sign with his finger.)* doolally.

TANNOY: Flight number 4678. British Airways to Berlin. Now boarding at gate nineteen. Can all passengers please proceed to gate nineteen.

KEVIN checks his watch.

KEVIN: They should be calling us soon.

CARLOS: Are we going somewhere?

KEVIN: Aye. We're gannin to Baghdad.

CARLOS: To Iraq?

KEVIN: *(Laughing.)* Aye. Baghdad's in Iraq. Well ye should knaa. It's your home toon.

CARLOS: What?

KEVIN: I said ye should knaa.

CARLOS: I don't understand you. Are you speaking English?

KEVIN: Ya cheeky bastard. What d'ya think I'm speaking? French?

CARLOS: *(Confused.)* But I don't understand French. Can you speak in English please?

KEVIN: I am speaking English! I'm English! Who the fuck are ye to tell me to speak in English?

CARLOS: I am sorry.

KEVIN: Aye, well. Just watch yesel'. That's all I'm sayin'.

CARLOS: Why are you taking me to Iraq?

KEVIN: Well we're gannin to Istanbul first. Three hours… *(Taking out tickets from his bag.)* Nearly four hours. Then we got a six-hour wait for the connection. Two and a half hours to Baghdad. That's… *(Counts on his fingers.)* We should be there by…

KEVIN looks at his watch and counts on his fingers. This goes on for several moments.

KEVIN: Tomorrow. When we get there.

CARLOS: Why are you taking me to Iraq?

KEVIN: Ya really don't remember nothin'? I should get some a them pills for me missus. She doesn't forget nowt that one. She's like the Million Dollar Man. Bionic memory. *(Slowly.)* You're getting deported. You're getting sent back to where you come from. I'm taking you home.

CARLOS: This is my home. I'm a British citizen.

KEVIN laughs.

CARLOS: I'm British.

KEVIN: Nah. You were a guest. But ya didn't behave yeself. The judge said you should be deported back to Iraq after you completed your prison sentence.

CARLOS: Prison?

KEVIN: Jesus, Salim! You attacked ya wife! Your wife? Remember?

CARLOS struggles to remember.

CARLOS: There must be a mistake. My name is Carlos Fuentes. Look. Let me show you. Where is my wallet? If you could take the handcuffs off so I can show you some ID.

KEVIN: Aye. Aye.

CARLOS: I'm telling you. There's been a mistake. I shouldn't be here.

KEVIN: I shouldn't be here either. Today was meant to be me day off.

CARLOS: No. Look. You've got the wrong guy. I'm Carlos Fuentes.

KEVIN laughs.

KEVIN: You're Carlos Fuentes are ya?

CARLOS: Yes.

KEVIN: Carlos Fuentes? That's ya real name is it?

CARLOS: Yes. I haven't done anything wrong. I'm innocent.

KEVIN: What haven't you done?

CARLOS: I… *(Struggles to remember.)* I don't know.

KEVIN: So how d'ya knaa you're innocent? Maybe you did something you cannat remember and now it's caught up with ya. Maybe it's karma.

CARLOS: I don't believe in karma.

KEVIN: You don't do ya? What do ya believe in?

CARLOS: I… I don't know.

KEVIN laughs.

CARLOS: Please. Just let me call someone.

KEVIN: Who ya gonna call?

CARLOS: I…the…police?

KEVIN laughs.

KEVIN: Like Judge Dredd said. I *am* the law.

CARLOS: You're a policeman?

KEVIN: Well. Nah. Not technically. I'm a security guard. The Home Office don't do this kinda donkey work themselves. They contract it out to private companies like mine. The good news is. I get six hours downtime in Baghdad after I've dropped you off. Now I checked the weather forecast on me phone. 41 degrees celsius in the shade. I've got me sun cream and me hat but still. It's gonna be roasting.

CARLOS: I want to go home.

KEVIN: I'm taking you home.

CARLOS: No. My home in London. I want to go home. I don't want to go to Iraq.

KEVIN: I'm afraid that's not possible.

CARLOS: I want to go home. Forty…forty-one Regent's Road. Forty-one Regent's Road… Primrose Hill. London. London NW1… NW1…four…4QD. 4QD. London 4QD!

KEVIN: You're not going home.

CARLOS: I want to go home. TAKE ME HOME!

KEVIN punches CARLOS on the side of his head. The punch is hard, but not hard enough to seriously injure or knock him over. CARLOS is more stunned by the sudden violence than hurt. He puts his hands up instinctively to protect his head.

Beat.

CARLOS lowers his hands slightly and opens his eyes.

Beat.

KEVIN sits back down in his seat. CARLOS lowers his hands. CARLOS looks at his left hand. He realises his ring is missing.

CARLOS looks at KEVIN.

KEVIN: Ya got somethin' to say?

CARLOS: Where is my ring?

KEVIN: What ring?

CARLOS: My wedding ring.

KEVIN shrugs.

KEVIN: Cannat help ya.

CARLOS: It's silver with a red stone. A bright red stone.

KEVIN: Haven't seen it.

CARLOS: Did you take it?

KEVIN: I'd be careful going round making accusations. It's a long flight. *(Beat.)* Now…

TANNOY: Lufthansa flight LU67 now boarding at gate thirty-four. Gate thirty-four.

KEVIN: Now what I need from you. Is some advice on what to see while I'm in Baghdad. I've only got a few hours before me flight home…

CARLOS: What's going to happen to me in Iraq?

KEVIN: I divn't knaa. My job's to hand ye over to the authorities. That's me done. You'll have to ask them. Nowt to dee with me. Now. I've had a look on Tripadvisor. *(Looking at his phone.)* There's only two reviews. Baghdad doesn't seem to be a very popular tourist destination. Shame you're not Turkish. I coulda had more time in Istanbul. Looks a lot more lively. And I heard the birds are alreet too. But em…what do you reckon? Shall I gan to the Iraq Museum or the Maximall?

CARLOS is lost in his thoughts not paying attention.

KEVIN: HERE! Wakey-wakey! Iraq Museum or Maximall? I haven't got time to do both. And I wanna get some decent pictures to stick on Facebook.

CARLOS: The Iraq Museum or the what?

KEVIN: The Maximall. Here. Hang on. I'll read ya the review. *(Reading from his phone. He reads slowly and stumbles over the occasional word.)* This isn't actually a mall. It is a four-storey department store which offers an experience like any Western department store. Clean, good fitting rooms and nice help. The food court on the top floor is clean and nice. Food offerings are the usual fast food crap. However there is one cafe where the atmosphere is truly lovely with modern (not tacky) decor and huge windows of what was going to be the biggest mosque in the world before construction stopped. In America, I avoid shopping and malls and departments like the plague, but I go here to just feel a slice of cleanliness in a city where there is still garbage and filth everywhere. *(Beat.)* Sounds alright. What d'ya reckon?

CARLOS: Sounds wonderful.

KEVIN: Well there's that or the museum. Shall I read ya the museum? I'll read ya the museum. *(Reading.)* I must say this museum *was* amazing. They had so much to see and discover but after the States invaded they pretty much took all the good stuff. I really think it was wrong, but there was nothing to do. The museum was really one of a kind! I hope it gets the same as it used to be! Aye. Sounds fucking shit. I'm gonna gan to the Maximall.

KEVIN sees CARLOS' head is bowed down towards the ground.

KEVIN: Salim. HOW! SALIM!

CARLOS looks up at KEVIN.

KEVIN: I thought you'd fallen asleep again.

CARLOS: No. I was. *(Beat.)* I was thinking.

KEVIN: Ah. Right. Well…

TANNOY: Turkish Airlines flight number 786 to Istanbul now boarding at gate one.

KEVIN: That's us.

KEVIN starts packing up the rucksack.

TANNOY: Turkish Airlines flight number 786 boarding at gate one.

KEVIN: Right. Well I'm gonna go for a dump before we get on the plane. I canna shit on planes. The air pressure. Plays havoc with me insides. D'ya wanna use the toilet before we set off?

CARLOS: No.

KEVIN: Alreet. Suit ya self. I'm gonna lock this door. You sit tight here and I'll be back in a jiffy.

KEVIN zips up the rucksack and places it on the table. He is about to leave when he stops and unzips the rucksack. KEVIN takes out CARLOS' ring from the bag. KEVIN holds up the ring so CARLOS can see it.

KEVIN: Divn't want to forget me ring. Cannat trust nee one these days.

KEVIN pockets the ring and leaves.

CARLOS looks at the rucksack. He opens the rucksack and rifles through it, emptying it of its contents. He finds a washbag and opens it up, sizing up each object before disregarding them. A toothbrush, a mini can of deodorant, a bar of soap are all taken out and thrown away.

CARLOS finds a biro pen. He takes off the lid and looks at the tip. CARLOS prepares to stab himself in the wrist. He lifts up the pen with his right hand and brings it down hard on his left wrist. He lets out a scream of pain.

CARLOS: AH! FUCK!

CARLOS looks at his left wrist. He has not even drawn blood. CARLOS throws the pen away. He looks in the bag again. He rifles through it until he finds a pair of shorts. The shorts have a leather belt attached. CARLOS removes the belt, pulls it to check the strength and then makes it into a loop.

CARLOS looks up at the ceiling. CARLOS stands up and climbs onto the chair. CARLOS places the belt loop around his neck.

TANNOY: This is a final call for Turkish Airlines flight number 786 to Istanbul.

CARLOS stops and looks upwards.

CARLOS: God?

Pause.

TANNOY: Turkish Airlines 786 to Istanbul now closing. Gate one.

CARLOS looks towards the door.

Beat.

CARLOS looks up.

Lights down slowly.

INTERLUDE 2

21 August 2008.

During the scene change SAHAR appears looking at her mobile phone, willing it to ring. She looks at the screen for several moments. She dials a number. It rings and rings and then goes through to voicemail.

SAHAR: *(Phone.)* Salim!? Where are you? I told you it was an emergency. Something terrible has happened. You must call me back straightaway. *(Beat.)* I am at the hospital. *(Beat.)* There was a bomb. She…

She starts to cry. She hangs up and walks offstage.

FIVE

June 2008.

Lydia's home. Bedroom. CARLOS, wearing a suit and tie, is sat on the edge of the bed. He is absorbed in an online computer game he is playing on a laptop. CARLOS is wearing headphones and laughing to himself.

LYDIA enters. She is getting ready to go out. She puts on her heels. She looks in the mirror as she checks her make-up.

CARLOS laughs loudly. He has a fairly strong Iraqi accent.

LYDIA: *(Turning.)* Sorry?

> *CARLOS is oblivious to her.*

LYDIA: Carlos?

> *CARLOS laughs loudly to a friend he is playing against online.*

CARLOS: *(To the laptop.)* You talk shit man. I blast you with bazooka in your face!

LYDIA: CARLOS!?

CARLOS: *(Looking up and taking an earphone out.)* Huh? Did you say something?

LYDIA: Are you ready? The taxi's outside.

CARLOS: Oh. *(To laptop.)* Hey, Afzal I have to go. What? Not if I see you first bitch. Ha! OK man.

> *CARLOS closes the laptop and stands up. LYDIA stares at CARLOS giving him the once over as she puts her earrings on.*

LYDIA: You're wearing that suit.

CARLOS: You said smart.

LYDIA: I said smart-casual. You're going to wear that jacket?

CARLOS: What is wrong with jacket?

LYDIA: *The.* What is wrong with *the* jacket? It looks...dowdy.

CARLOS: What is dow-dee?

LYDIA: Frumpy.

CARLOS: I don't know this word either.

LYDIA: Shit! It looks shit. I've been telling you to get a decent jacket for over a year.

CARLOS: This is good quality jacket. It is British Home Stores. Look.

He tries to show her the label. She bats him away.

LYDIA: Carlos. How many times have I told you just because it's called British doesn't make it good? That jacket looks like you got it off a blind, geriatric tramp who's let himself go.

Beat.

CARLOS takes off the jacket. LYDIA looks at him.

LYDIA: And the tie please.

CARLOS: What is wrong with tie?

LYDIA: You can't wear a tie without a jacket.

CARLOS: Who say?

LYDIA: I do. It's not done.

A stand-off.

LYDIA: Carlos. One of us is an expert in corporate rebranding. Responsible for multi-million pound accounts, advising some of the biggest companies on earth on how to present themselves to the public. How to talk, think and act. *(Beat.)* The other person is you.

CARLOS: Maybe you do not know what is best for me.

LYDIA: Do you want to look like a waiter in a Lebanese restaurant?

Beat.

CARLOS takes off the tie. He looks to her for approval. LYDIA walks over to him and undoes his top button, looks at the effect, then undoes another button.

CARLOS: Happy?

LYDIA: You look so stiff. Try rolling up your shirt sleeves.

CARLOS wearily does as she instructs.

CARLOS: Can we go now?

LYDIA: Can't you do anything with the hair?

She comes up to him and ruffles his hair affectionately. She smiles. He smiles.

CARLOS goes to kiss her, but she pulls away. He looks hurt, but she smiles.

LYDIA: Make-up. Don't want to get it smudged.

CARLOS: Ah. I thought maybe you are shamed by me.

LYDIA: A-shamed. *(Beat.)* Don't forget everything we've worked so hard on darling.

LYDIA picks up her handbag and looks at CARLOS with a sense of trepidation.

LYDIA: Right. *(Beat.)* Ready?

CARLOS: Yes.

CARLOS takes out his silver ring with the bright red stone from his pocket and puts it on.

LYDIA: For God's sake don't wear that ring Carlos.

CARLOS: It is my ring.

LYDIA: You can't wear that. It's hideous.

CARLOS: I like my ring.

LYDIA: It looks like a flying saucer.

CARLOS: No one will be looking at my ring at a party.

LYDIA: It's a *dinner* party. And *everyone* will be looking at it in case it takes off.

CARLOS: I'm wearing the ring.

LYDIA: Carlos.

CARLOS: Go without me.

LYDIA: I can't turn up on my own. I told Franny and Tim you were coming.

CARLOS: I come with ring or not.

LYDIA: You're going to do this now?

CARLOS: Maybe it is best I stay at home if you are a-shamed by me.

LYDIA: *My* home.

CARLOS: They are not *my* friends. They are *your* friends.

LYDIA: Who are waiting to meet you. Waiting to meet the wonderful, exotic, *younger* man I've been telling them about.

CARLOS: Really?

LYDIA: Yes. Don't make me go on my own. *Please.*

CARLOS: I am a man.

LYDIA: Nobody's disputing that.

CARLOS: You push me too far Lydia.

LYDIA: You said you wanted my help. That's all I'm doing.

CARLOS: But the way you talk to me.

LYDIA: How?

CARLOS: I don't think you talked to your ex-husband like this.

LYDIA: You don't know what you're talking about Carlos. My ex-husband was *nothing* like you. He was a waste of space.

CARLOS: Waste?

LYDIA: He was weak. Lazy. A liar. A...philanderer. *(CARLOS doesn't understand the word.)* Somebody who cheats on people.

CARLOS: Cheat you? From money?

LYDIA: No. A philanderer is...he slept with other women. *(Beat.)* Behind my back. Sex.

CARLOS: Oh! Intercourse.

LYDIA: Yes. He was one of those failed artist types. Big dreams but little talent for anything other than sponging off me. *You're* not him. You've got ambition. Drive. You...you're... *different.*

CARLOS: I don't want to different. I want to be...

LYDIA: British. Yes, I know…

CARLOS: No. I don't know. Maybe. What. What if I can not be British like you want me to be?

LYDIA: I like you just the way you are. *(Smiling.)* With a few minor adjustments

CARLOS: This ring is all I have. I have no friends. No job. I stay home all day waiting for you to come.

LYDIA: Darling, I'm not stopping you from getting a job. Making friends. I want you to be happy. And it's not true. You've got me. What do you want? Tell me. Whatever you want. I'll get it for you.

CARLOS smiles. LYDIA smiles.

CARLOS: Anything I want Ms King?

LYDIA: Anything you want Mr Fuentes.

They embrace. A tender moment between them.

LYDIA: Just tell me why the ring's so important to you.

As quietly as possible SAHAR enters wearing a short blue dress. CARLOS can see her. LYDIA can't. SAHAR and LYDIA speak at the same time with their words overlapping.

SAHAR: Tell her.   LYDIA: Carlos?

CARLOS looks at SAHAR.

SAHAR: Tell her what it means.

CARLOS: I can not.

LYDIA: You can't do what?

SAHAR: Tell her about me.   LYDIA: Carlos? What can't you do?

SAHAR: The wife and child you left behind.

CARLOS: *(Looking at SAHAR.)* She won't understand.

LYDIA: Understand what?

SAHAR: Are you afraid she will throw you out? There is nothing left for you in Iraq.

CARLOS: Iraq is my home.   LYDIA: What are you talking
                                about?

SAHAR: There is nothing for Carlos. That is who you are now.
Salim is dead.

SAHAR starts to leave.

CARLOS: Salim is not dead.

LYDIA: Who?

SAHAR exits.

CARLOS: *(After SAHAR.)* Salim is not dead!

LYDIA: Who is Salim? Who are you talking to?

CARLOS: *(After SAHAR, not to LYDIA.)* Salim is alive! You must
believe me!

LYDIA: Carlos?

CARLOS: *(After SAHAR.)* I am not dead. I am Salim Abdul
Husain. From Baghdad. From Iraq. I am not *dead.* I am a
Sunni, you are a Shia. *I* am not dead. My wife, my child.
I am *not* dead. Please. *(Crying.)* You must believe me. You
must not forget. I am not dead. I… I am…not…

LYDIA: Carlos? Carlos darling? You're scaring me.

CARLOS: *(Crying.)* Please. Come back. COME BACK!

LYDIA comforts CARLOS as he calls after SAHAR.

CARLOS: Don't go!

LYDIA: I'm right here. I'm not going anywhere.

CARLOS looks at LYDIA. She soothes him.

LYDIA: I'm here.

Lights down.

INTERLUDE 3

22 August 2008.

SAHAR enters with a mobile phone to her ear.

SAHAR: *(Phone.)* She had no breakfast. Nothing. I told her
I said you have to eat. Eat something. If you don't eat I
won't let you go to school. *(Beat.)* They told me not to
look. The doctor. Advised me. Strongly. We strongly advise
you not to look. *(Pause.)* She was wearing the white vest.
The white one with the blue flowers. You remember? The
one that you sent her. It was her favourite. She was wearing
that under her clothes. What was left…it was all I could…
the blue flower. Blue and white. *(Beat.)* And red. Blood.
So much. Her…face was…metal… glass. Her eyes. Arms.
Fingers. The blue flower. Look at the blue flower. *(Beat.)*
She had no breakfast. *(Pause.)* Who kills a child on her
way to school? *(Pause.)* Did you hear what I said? *(Pause.)*
Salim? *(Beat.)* Yes. *(Beat.)* Yes. *(Beat.)* Yes. *(Pause.)* The
funeral was this afternoon. I didn't think you would come.
So we didn't wait.

Lights down slowly.

SIX

April 2006.

Baghdad. Street market. KHALED, in overalls, is cleaning up the aftermath of an explosion. He sweeps slowly and cautiously with a broom, on the lookout for body parts and valuables. There are two bin bags centre stage. One is black, the other is yellow.

CARLOS: *(Off, in Arabic.)* Where's my broom?

KHALED: *(Arabic.)* How should I know? Look in the van.

CARLOS: *(Off, Arabic.)* I'm looking in the van.

    Pause.

KHALED: *(English.)* Found it? *(Beat.)* Hey Camel-face!?

CARLOS: *(Off.)* What?

KHALED: Did you find your broom?

CARLOS: *(Off.)* Yes.

    CARLOS, in overalls, enters with his broom.

KHALED: By the way, the next valuable we find is mine.

CARLOS: The next valuable *I* find is mine.

KHALED: What about the wallet*?*

CARLOS: The empty wallet?

KHALED: A wallet is a wallet.

CARLOS: Not if there's nothing in it.

KHALED: It's still a valuable.

CARLOS: How the fuck is it a valuable when there's nothing valuable in it?

KHALED: That's the rule.

CARLOS: What rule? I didn't see that rule.

KHALED: It's an unwritten rule.

CARLOS: Fuck off. You're making it up. They don't have rules about what valuables you can steal when you're cleaning up body parts after a bomb goes off. They don't 'write' rules for that kind of thing.

KHALED: That's why it's an unwritten rule.

CARLOS: Unwrite my balls.

KHALED: You'd love that wouldn't you? You filthy bastard.

CARLOS: OK. I tell you what. Why don't we trade the empty wallet for the gold chain?

KHALED: Trade?

CARLOS: Yeah. Y'know? The gold chain I found this morning that you took. And I'll give you back the empty wallet that you found.

KHALED: Nah. I'm…there's no trading here. It's an unwritten rule.

CARLOS: Where's this book of rules?

KHALED: It's not written.

CARLOS: Oh fucking surprise, surprise.

KHALED: This isn't the United Nations Salim! We work for the Baghdad Municipal Street Cleaning Department. We do things by the book. And if you don't like it, I suggest you take it up with George Bush. The next time you're blowing him on his cowboy ranch in Texas.

CARLOS: That's disgusting. Me. Blowing the President of the United States. Do you really think I'd suck off George Bush? *(Beat.)* Bill Clinton maybe.

KHALED laughs. CARLOS smiles. They go back to sweeping.

CARLOS walks over to the yellow bin bag to empty his dustpan.

KHALED: Hey!

CARLOS stops.

KHALED: What are you doing? The black one. Yellow for body parts. Black for general waste. How many times do I have to tell you?

CARLOS empties the dustpan in the black bag.

KHALED: You need to listen. If you don't listen, you don't learn. And if you don't learn, you don't get ahead. Don't you want to get ahead?

CARLOS: As a road sweeper? Not really.

KHALED: You've got no ambition have you? A road sweeper today. Yeah. But tomorrow a road sweeper supervisor. A road sweeper director. You could be overseeing the whole of Baghdad's sweeping needs.

CARLOS: I'm happy doing what I'm doing.

KHALED: Cleaning up body parts and burnt vegetables?

CARLOS: It's steady work.

KHALED: Look at me. I'm not going to be a road sweeper forever. No way Mohammed. As soon as I get the money for a visa I'm off. Goodbye. You'll come into work one day and ask where's Khaled? And they'll say, oh haven't you heard? Khaled got a visa. He's gone to Amreeka. *(Waves.)* Bye-Bye motherfuckers.

CARLOS: Amreeka?

KHALED: Yes. Khaled al-Hamrani. American. US baby.

KHALED makes the peace sign with his hand. CARLOS smiles.

KHALED: What?

CARLOS chuckles to himself.

KHALED: What's so funny?

CARLOS tries to suppress a laugh and compose himself.

CARLOS: Oh, nothing. Nothing.

CARLOS shakes his head.

KHALED: You'd rather stay here? Get blown up buying aubergines like the poor fuckers in this market?

CARLOS: An American? Come on.

KHALED: Better than being an Iraqi. How can you be an Iraqi when there is no Iraq? The best thing an ambitious young man can do is leave.

CARLOS: If we all leave then who's gonna build the country back up?

KHALED: Who cares? This country is finished. There's nothing here but death. You either die fast or you die slow. Either way you die.

CARLOS: What about your family? You'd leave them behind?

KHALED: I'm better off to them alive somewhere else sending money back than staying here and being dead. It'll be our corpses somebody else is cleaning up. Oh. What's this? What's this teeny-weeny little thing that I can barely see that looks like a pickled vegetable? Oh that's right. It's Salim's cock.

CARLOS smirks and shakes his head. KHALED walks over to the black bag to empty his dustpan.

CARLOS: How would you go about getting a visa to America? *(Beat.)* Hypothetically.

KHALED leans in conspiratorially.

KHALED: Between you and me?

CARLOS nods.

KHALED: I know a guy. Who knows a guy. Who knows a guy. He. Is a Major-General in the US Army. He. Writes you a letter. That says you have courageously and honourably served the US Armed Forces in Iraq as an interpreter. And that as a result of your invaluable translation services for the American Government your life is now in danger. This letter then gets sent to the US State Department along with your application for a SIV.

CARLOS: You've got a broom. Why do you want a sieve?

KHALED: A SIV! An S-I-V. A Special Immigrant Visa. *(Beat.)* It's a fucking green card for the USA.

CARLOS: An interpreter?

KHALED: Yeah.

CARLOS: You?

KHALED: Yeah. Why?

CARLOS: Your English is shit.

KHALED: Fuck off! My English is excellent.

55

CARLOS: You learned English from watching Arnold Schwarzenegger movies.

KHALED: So?

CARLOS: You learned English from someone who can't speak English. He's Austrian!

KHALED: No. He's not. He *was* an Austrian. *Now* he's an American. He's The Governator! That's the great thing about America. Anyone can be an American.

CARLOS: Even you? And how much do one of these letters cost?

Beat.

KHALED: Twenty thousand dollars.

CARLOS: Twenty grand! That's a lot of money.

KHALED: Yes. It is.

KHALED ties up the black bag because it is full.

KHALED: Inshallah. (God willing.)

CARLOS: Inshallah.

KHALED carries the black bag off. CARLOS resumes sweeping. He bends down and picks up something from the floor.

CARLOS stands up to look at the object. It is a human finger with a large silver ring on it. It is set with a red stone that sparkles brightly. CARLOS removes the ring from the finger with some difficulty. He inspects the ring, holding it up to the sky.

CARLOS puts the ring on his own finger and admires it. He throws the finger into the yellow bag.

KHALED: *(Off.)* SALIM!

CARLOS tries to take the ring off. He can't. He moves upstage and turns his back as he tries to pull the ring off.

KHALED: *(Off.)* SALIM! SOMEONE HERE TO SEE YOU!

CARLOS tries to yank the ring off. Footsteps. KHALED enters followed by SAHAR, she is dressed in an abaya and has her face covered by a niqab.

CARLOS has his back to them.

KHALED: Salim…

In that same moment CARLOS succeeds in yanking off the ring. He looks at it, without the other two seeing it, and smiles.

KHALED: Your wife is here to see you.

CARLOS looks back over his shoulder. His smile evaporates. CARLOS pockets the ring and turns his body to face SAHAR.

CARLOS: What are you doing here?

SAHAR looks over at KHALED.

CARLOS: *(To KHALED.)* Can you……

KHALED walks off.

CARLOS: You came here alone?

SAHAR looks back over her shoulder.

CARLOS: He's gone.

SAHAR takes off her niqab to reveal her face.

CARLOS: You shouldn't have come here alone.

SAHAR: Don't tell me what to do.

CARLOS: It's not safe for a woman.

SAHAR: Where is safe?

Beat.

CARLOS: What happened?

SAHAR: What they warned you would happen.

CARLOS: What?… Did they?…

He touches her face.

SAHAR: No. My father was home.

CARLOS: Who was it?

SAHAR: I don't know.

CARLOS: What did they look like?

SAHAR: I don't know. They all look the same. Angry young men with guns.

CARLOS: What did they do?

SAHAR: They beat my father. I had to listen to them beat him. I was hiding on the roof with Lina. Trying to stop her from crying. An old man begging for mercy while they kicked him and punched him. Spat on him. Called him a dog. A traitor. My father. And I could do nothing to help him.

CARLOS: How is he?

SAHAR: Oh he's great! Couldn't be better. How do you think!?

CARLOS: What about Lina? Where is she?

SAHAR: She's with my mother.

CARLOS: And you? Are you OK?

SAHAR: OK? NO! I'M NOT OK! I'm not OK at all. They told you to leave. They warned you a Sunni can not live in a Shia neighbourhood.

CARLOS: This is my home! Why should I leave?

SAHAR: A Sunni can not be married to a Shia.

CARLOS: I am a Muslim and you are a Muslim. That is all that matters.

SAHAR: Not anymore. Not since Saddam. Not to them. They warned you. They told you what they'd do. But you wouldn't listen. This is your fault. This is all your fault.

SAHAR starts to cry. CARLOS tries to comfort her, but she shrugs him off aggressively.

SAHAR: Don't!

CARLOS: It's OK.

SAHAR: It's not OK.

CARLOS touches her arm.

CARLOS: Please.

SAHAR: Don't touch me.

SAHAR shrugs him off.

SAHAR: Don't ever touch me!

CARLOS: Please Sahar. I'm sorry. Forgive me. We'll go to another neighbourhood. Somewhere safe.

SAHAR: There is nowhere safe for a Shia and a Sunni in Iraq.

CARLOS: You're my wife! I will not leave you. I will not leave my daughter. We are a family. If we have to leave Iraq, if we have to go to the ends of the earth, so that we can be safe. So that we can be together as a family, then that is what we must do.

SAHAR: Salim! They will come back and they will kill you. And they will kill me. And they will kill our daughter.

CARLOS: I will fight them.

SAHAR: With what? Your broom? Are you going to sweep them away?

CARLOS: I'm not going without you and Lina.

SAHAR: Lina is five years old. How can she go anywhere? My parents are old. My father is sick. They have no one else to care for them. I will not abandon them. You must go. Salim. Please. I have packed a bag for you. My father…

SAHAR reaches into the bag and takes out a wedge of US dollars tied together by a rubber band.

SAHAR: It will not get you to America. But Europe maybe. Your cousin in London…

CARLOS: I can't take that.

SAHAR: Take it!

CARLOS: What will you do without a husband? Lina without a father? It is too dangerous for a woman on her own.

SAHAR: I will be safer without you.

CARLOS looks at the money.

SAHAR: Please. Salim. If you have ever loved me then do this for me. I have obeyed you as a wife. I am asking you now to obey me. A Sunni can not be married to a Shia.

Pause.

CARLOS takes the money and the bag from SAHAR.

CARLOS: I will send for you.

SAHAR: No.

CARLOS: As soon as I can. You and Lina.

SAHAR: No. I will not wait for you. You must go and not come back. That is the only way we will be safe.

Pause.

CARLOS picks up the bag.

Beat.

He puts the bag down and reaches into his pocket for the ring. He walks over to SAHAR and gives her the ring.

CARLOS: Here. Keep it or sell it if you can get a good price.

SAHAR examines the ring slowly.

SAHAR: It's a fake.

CARLOS holds the ring up to the light.

CARLOS: Are you sure?

SAHAR: It's not worth anything. *(Beat.)* Why don't you give me your wedding ring instead?

Pause.

CARLOS takes off his wedding ring slowly and gives it to SAHAR. He looks into her eyes.

CARLOS: I divorce you. I divorce you. I divorce you.

SAHAR takes the fake ring from CARLOS and solemnly puts it on his finger. She kisses CARLOS gently.

SAHAR: Thank you.

Pause.

SAHAR puts her niqab on and leaves.

CARLOS looks at his ring.

Beat.

He picks up his bag.

Lights down.

SEVEN

January 2009.

Lydia's home. Bedroom. CARLOS, dressed in a white T-shirt and boxer shorts, is sat up in bed. His hands are handcuffed to the bedpost. LYDIA, wearing a slip, is on her hands and knees looking for something on the floor.

CARLOS points to a spot on the floor with his foot. He is wearing his ring and has a moderate Iraqi accent.

CARLOS: Over there.

LYDIA: Where?

CARLOS: *(Pointing.)* There.

    She looks to where he is pointing.

LYDIA: Here?

CARLOS: No. *(His foot can't reach so he indicates with his eyes.)* Look.

LYDIA: *(Looking on the floor.)* I can't see it.

CARLOS: Look eyes!

LYDIA: What do you think I'm looking with? I can't see the pill. How did you drop it? I'll have to go and get you another one.

CARLOS: No. Sahar look!

LYDIA: Who?

    LYDIA gets up.

CARLOS: What?

LYDIA: What did you just call me?

CARLOS: Call you what?

LYDIA: You called me Sahar.

CARLOS: I did? But you are not Sahar.

LYDIA: I know I'm not Sahar! It's bad enough you can't remember you attacked me last night. You can at least try and remember my name.

CARLOS: I know your name. You are…you are…

LYDIA: Your *wife*. Your *second* wife.

CARLOS: Yes. You are…You are my *second* wife. *(Beat.)* Lydia.

LYDIA: Well done.

CARLOS: This is why you handcuff me Lydia? Because I can't remember your name? This is not very nice.

LYDIA: *(Snaps.)* No! I handcuffed you because you tried to bloody strangle me!

CARLOS: I did?

LYDIA: Yes!

CARLOS: But I don't remember.

LYDIA: You don't remember?

CARLOS: No. Ah, maybe it was a nightmare.

LYDIA stares at CARLOS.

CARLOS: What? Why are you accusing me like this?

LYDIA: I'm going to get the pills.

LYDIA starts to leave.

CARLOS: Lydia?

LYDIA looks back.

The handcuffs?

Beat.

LYDIA: I'll get the medicine first.

She leaves.

Pause.

CARLOS: Lydia? *(Beat.)* LYDIA? *(Pause.)* LYDIA!?

LYDIA enters carrying a large bottle of water and a plastic glass. She pours out a glass of water.

LYDIA: Here you go.

LYDIA reveals she has a white pill in her hand. She tries to feed it to CARLOS, but he turns his head away.

LYDIA: Take the pill.

CARLOS looks at her suspiciously.

LYDIA: Open your mouth.

CARLOS: What is this?

LYDIA: It's medicine. For your nightmares. To stop you having the bad dreams.

CARLOS looks at the pill.

CARLOS: I don't want it.

LYDIA: You have to. It's the only way we can control the nightmares.

CARLOS: No!

LYDIA: *(Smiling.)* Take the pill Salim. Please. Take it for me.

LYDIA tries to feed him the pill, but CARLOS turns his head away.

CARLOS: I am not Salim! I'm Carlos… Carlos Fuentes.

LYDIA: No. You're not.

CARLOS: I am Carlos.

LYDIA: No.

CARLOS: I'm Carlos!

LYDIA: Salim!

CARLOS: Carlos!

LYDIA: Carlos isn't real. You're Salim Abdul Husain. From Baghdad. From Iraq. A Sunni not a Shia. Remember? You told me.

CARLOS: *(Confused.)* No.

LYDIA: You're Salim Abdul Husain.

CARLOS: Salim?

LYDIA: Yes.

CARLOS looks confused.

LYDIA: You don't remember do you?

CARLOS shakes his head.

LYDIA: You tried to jump out of the window. You tried to kill yourself. We have to make sure you don't hurt anybody. You. Or me. Otherwise we'll have to take you back to that place. And I don't want that to happen. Let me look after you.

LYDIA tries to give CARLOS the pill, but he knocks her hand sending the glass of water flying.

LYDIA looks at CARLOS angrily. She grabs his head and tries to open his mouth, he struggles but eventually she manages to prise it open and force the pill in. She shuts his mouth.

LYDIA picks up the glass from the floor and refills it with water. She offers it to CARLOS. He pulls at his handcuffs.

CARLOS: The handcuffs?

LYDIA takes out a key and unlocks the handcuffs. CARLOS looks at her warily. She smiles reassuringly.

LYDIA: Let's try again. OK?

LYDIA offers the glass of water. CARLOS takes the glass.

Beat.

CARLOS spits out the pill from his mouth and throws the water over LYDIA. He jumps up and grabs her around the throat.

LYDIA: Let me go! *(Beat.)* Please Salim. You're hurting me.

Pause.

CARLOS lets go of her throat.

CARLOS: Where is our daughter? Where is she? She's going to be late for school. You better call her for breakfast Sahar. *(Beat.)* What's the matter? Where's Lina? When's she coming?

Beat.

LYDIA: Lina's not coming.

CARLOS: Why? Where is she?

Beat.

LYDIA: She's dead.

CARLOS: No. That's not true. Where is Lina?

LYDIA: I know it's hard. But Lina's dead. *(Beat.)* And so is Sahar.

CARLOS: *(Disbelieving.)* No.

LYDIA: She's dead. Lina was killed by a car bomb in Baghdad. Sahar… Sahar committed suicide. *(Beat.)* I'm sorry.

CARLOS: No. That was a nightmare. It wasn't real. It was a dream.

LYDIA: This is real.

CARLOS: No.

LYDIA: This is real. I'm real. I'm your wife. You're my husband. We're married.

CARLOS: This isn't a nightmare?

LYDIA: No.

Pause.

LYDIA: Take the medicine Salim. It's the only way we can live together.

Pause.

CARLOS looks to the pill on the floor. Beat. He picks it up. LYDIA pours another glass of water. She holds it out to CARLOS. Beat. He takes the glass. CARLOS swallows the pill and washes it down with the water.

Beat.

LYDIA: Good.

Beat.

CARLOS: I… I feel tired.

LYDIA: Why don't you lie down then? Rest for a little bit.

CARLOS gets into bed.

CARLOS: Will you lie next to me?

LYDIA nods. She gets into bed with CARLOS. He rests his head on her. She strokes his hair.

CARLOS: Do you remember the day we first met?

LYDIA: Yes. In the restaurant.

CARLOS: No. *(Beat.)* It was the park.

LYDIA: The park?

CARLOS: Yes. In Baghdad

LYDIA: Oh. The park.

CARLOS: Yes. You were sitting in the park.

> *Beat.*

LYDIA: I was eating my lunch?

CARLOS: Yes. Correct.

LYDIA: I was eating my lunch in the park.

CARLOS: Good. Do you remember what you were wearing?

> *Beat.*

LYDIA: A skirt?

CARLOS: A dress. A short blue dress. *(Smiling.)* It showed off your legs.

LYDIA: Oh. How could I forget?

> *Beat.*

CARLOS: What were you doing? In the park?

> *Beat.*

LYDIA: I was trying to read my book.

CARLOS: You weren't really reading though were you?

LYDIA: No. I was trying not to look over at you. You were talking to your friends.

CARLOS: No. I was playing football with my friends. *(Beat.)* What was it I said when I came over to you?

LYDIA: You said the stupidest thing.

CARLOS: *(Smiling.)* Did I? Oh yeah! I did, didn't I? God! *(Beat.)* Remind me what I said Sahar.

> *Beat.*

LYDIA: Can I borrow some of your grass please?

CARLOS laughs.

CARLOS: What a... I was so nervous. It was the first thing that came into my head.

LYDIA: I could tell you were nervous.

CARLOS: But you weren't. You were so confident and poised. So elegant. That's what attracted me to you. You were different from all the other girls. That's when I fell in love with you.

LYDIA: Right away?

CARLOS: Yes. The very first time I saw you.

LYDIA ruffles his hair affectionately.

CARLOS: Sahar?

LYDIA: Yes?

CARLOS: I love you.

LYDIA: I love you too Salim.

CARLOS: Is Lina coming?

LYDIA: Yes.

CARLOS: I feel so tired.

LYDIA: Why don't you go to sleep then?

LYDIA gets out of the bed. CARLOS looks very sleepy.

CARLOS: Will you wake me up when she comes home?

LYDIA: Yes my love.

CARLOS picks up the handcuffs and looks at them.

It's for your own good.

Beat.

CARLOS holds out the handcuffs to LYDIA. She takes them and handcuffs him to the bed. CARLOS looks to her.

Go to sleep. I'll watch over you.

Beat.

CARLOS goes to sleep. LYDIA watches over him.

Lights down.

The End.